My SPANISH
Sticker Dictionary

Catherine Bruzzone and Louise Millar

Illustrations by Louise Comfort
Spanish adviser: María Concejo

b small publishing
www.bsmall.co.uk

En el zoo

en el thoh

giraffe

el elefante

el eleh-<u>fan</u>-teh

polar bear

crocodile

At the zoo

lion

tiger

el hipopótamo
el eepo-<u>pot</u>-am-o

snake

dolphin

Put a '¡bravo!' sticker here when you complete the page.

Can you find all the stickers?

car

la bicicleta
la bee-thee-<u>klet</u>-a

Find these vehicles in the big picture. Join them up with a line.

lorry

street

el semáforo
el se<u>mah</u>-foro

police car

bus stop

pavement

bus

Put a '¡bravo!' sticker here when you complete the page.

En el bosque

en el <u>bos</u>-keh

la mariposa

la maree-<u>poh</u>-sa

squirrel

deer

beetle

In the forest

fox

brown bear

la oruga
la or<u>oo</u>-ga

fly

rabbit

Put a '¡bravo!' sticker here when you complete the page.

En clase

en <u>klass</u>-eh

Find these things in the big picture. Join them up with a line.

teacher

glue

Can you find all the stickers?

book

la mesa

la <u>mess</u>a

la acera
la ah-<u>thair</u>-a

la profesora
la profes<u>sor</u>-a

el mango
el <u>mang</u>o

el pegamento
el peg-a<u>men</u>to

la piña
la <u>peen</u>-ya

el calabacín
el kalah-bah-<u>theen</u>

las uvas
lass <u>oo</u>bass

el conejo
el kon-<u>eh</u>-ho

la mosca
la <u>moss</u>-ka

la pasta
la <u>pas</u>-ta

el oso polar
el osso pol-<u>lar</u>

la berenjena
la bairen-<u>hay</u>-na

el autobús
el ah-oto-<u>boos</u>

el papel
el pap-<u>el</u>

el coche
el <u>ko</u>cheh

la jirafa
la hee-<u>rah</u>-fa

la mantequilla
la manteh-<u>kee</u>-ya

el ciervo
el thee-<u>air</u>-bo

la parada
la p<u>arah</u>-da

la patata
la pat-<u>ah</u>-ta

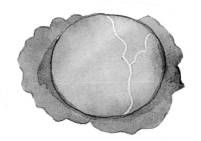

la col
la kol

la carne
la <u>kar</u>-neh

el camión
el kamy-<u>on</u>

la pluma
la <u>ploo</u>ma

el melocotón
el melo-ko-<u>ton</u>

la calle
la <u>kah</u>-yeh

el arroz
el ah-<u>roth</u>

la silla
la <u>see</u>-ya

la ardilla
la ar<u>dee</u>-ya

el tigre
el <u>tee</u>-greh

el huevo
el <u>way</u>-bo

la lechuga
la leh-<u>choo</u>-ga

la cereza
la theh-<u>reh</u>-tha

el escarabajo
el eskah-rah-<u>bah</u>-ho

el león
el lay-<u>on</u>

el coche
de policía
el <u>ko</u>cheh
deh polee-<u>thee</u>-ya

Have fun finding where these stickers belong.

¡bravo!

¡bravo!

¡bravo!

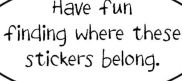

¡bravo!

¡bravo!

¡bravo!

¡bravo!

el maíz
el mah-<u>eeth</u>

el oso
pardo
el <u>oh</u>-so pardo

el cocodrilo
el kokko-<u>dree</u>-lo

el zorro
el <u>thoh</u>-roh

el lápiz
de color
el <u>lap</u>-eeth
deh kol-<u>or</u>

el libro
el <u>lee</u>bro

el plátano
el <u>plah</u>-tan-o

la leche
la <u>leh</u>-cheh

el delfín
el del-<u>feen</u>

el apio
el <u>ah</u>-pee-o

la serpiente
la sairp-<u>yen</u>-teh

el azúcar
el as-<u>thoo</u>-kar

la naranja
la nah-<u>ran</u>-ha

In the classroom

chair

el ordenador
el ordenad-<u>dor</u>

paper

coloured pencil

pen

Put a '¡bravo!' sticker here when you complete the page.

En el supermercado
en el soopair-mair-<u>kah</u>-do

Can you find all the stickers?

meat

butter

Find these foods in the big picture. Join them up with a line.

el pan
el pan

pasta

At the supermarket

rice

milk

sugar

egg

el pescado
el pes<u>kah</u>-doh

Put a '¡bravo!' sticker here when you complete the page.

En el huerto
en el oo-<u>air</u>-toh

Can you find all the stickers?

potato

cabbage

la zanahoria
la thanah-<u>or</u>-ee-a

courgette

Find these vegetables in the big picture. Join them up with a line.

In the vegetable garden

el tomate
el tom-*ah*-teh

lettuce

corn

celery

aubergine

Put a '¡bravo!' sticker here when you complete the page.

En el puesto de fruta
en el <u>pwes</u>to deh <u>froo</u>ta

Find these fruit in the big picture. Join them up with a line.

grapes

la manzana
la man-<u>thah</u>-na

Can you find all the stickers?

banana

mango

At the fruit stall

peach

pineapple

orange

la fresa
la <u>fray</u>-sa

cherry

Put a '¡bravo!' sticker here when you complete the page.

Lista de palabras
leesta deh pal-ab-rass

Word list

Spanish/español – English/inglés

la acera pavement
el apio celery
la ardilla squirrel
el arroz rice
el autobús bus
el azúcar sugar
la berenjena aubergine
la bicicleta bicycle
el bosque forest
el calabacín courgette
la calle street
el camión lorry
la carne meat
la cereza cherry
el ciervo deer
la clase classroom
el coche car
el coche de policía police car
el cocodrilo crocodile
la col cabbage
el conejo rabbit
el delfín dolphin
el elefante elephant
el escarabajo beetle
la fresa strawberry
la fruta fruit
el hipopótamo hippopotamus
el huerto vegetable garden
el huevo egg
la jirafa giraffe
el lápiz de color coloured pencil
la leche milk
la lechuga lettuce
el león lion

el libro book
el maíz corn
el mango mango
la mantequilla butter
la manzana apple
la mariposa butterfly
el melocotón peach
la mesa table
la mosca fly
la naranja orange (fruit)
el ordenador computer
la oruga caterpillar
el oso pardo brown bear
el oso polar polar bear
el pan bread
el papel paper
la parada bus stop
la pasta pasta
la patata potato
el pegamento glue
el pescado fish (to eat)
la piña pineapple
el plátano banana
la pluma pen
la profesora teacher
el puesto stall
el semáforo traffic lights
la serpiente snake
la silla chair
el supermercado supermarket
el tigre tiger
el tomate tomato
las uvas grapes
las verduras vegetables
la zanahoria carrot
el zoo zoo
el zorro fox

English/inglés – Spanish/español

apple la manzana
aubergine la berenjena
banana el plátano
beetle el escarabajo
bicycle la bicicleta
book el libro
bread el pan
brown bear el oso pardo
bus el autobús
bus stop la parada
butter la mantequilla
butterfly la mariposa
cabbage la col
car el coche
carrot la zanahoria
caterpillar la oruga
celery el apio
chair la silla
cherry la cereza
classroom la clase
coloured pencil el lápiz de color
computer el ordenador
corn el maíz
courgette el calabacín
crocodile el cocodrilo
deer el ciervo
dolphin el delfín
egg el huevo
elephant el elefante
fish (to eat) el pescado
fly la mosca
forest el bosque
fox el zorro
fruit la fruta
giraffe la jirafa
glue el pegamento
grapes las uvas

hippopotamus el hipopótamo
lettuce la lechuga
lion el león
lorry el camión
mango el mango
meat la carne
milk la leche
orange (fruit) la naranja
paper el papel
pasta la pasta
pavement la acera
peach el melocotón
pen la pluma
pineapple la piña
polar bear el oso polar
police car el coche de policía
potato la patata
rabbit el conejo
rice el arroz
snake la serpiente
squirrel la ardilla
stall el puesto
strawberry la fresa
street la calle
sugar el azúcar
supermarket el supermercado
table la mesa
teacher la profesora
tiger el tigre
tomato el tomate
traffic lights el semáforo
vegetable garden el huerto
vegetables las verduras
zoo el zoo

© b small publishing ltd. 2012

www.bsmall.co.uk www.facebook.co.uk/bsmallpublishing www.twitter.com/bsmallbear
ISBN: 978-1-908164-25-4

3 4 5

Editorial: Catherine Bruzzone, Louise Millar and Susan Martineau Design: Louise Millar Production: Madeleine Ehm
Printed in China by WKT Co. Ltd.